GREAT ZIMBABWE

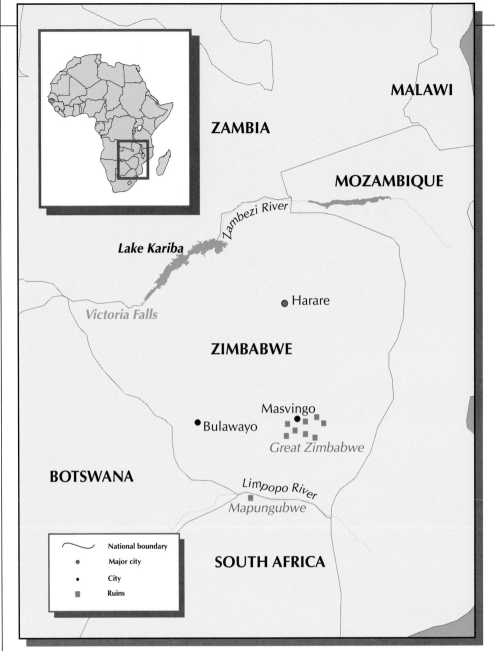

The capital of Great Zimbabwe was the largest city in southern Africa at the time.

~African Civilizations~

GREAT ZIMBABWE

Mark Bessire

A First Book

Franklin Watts
A Division of Grolier Publishing
New York / London / Hong Kong / Sydney
Danbury, Connecticut

Cover photograph copyright ©: Collection Marc and Denyse
Ginzberg/Solomon R. Guggenheim Museum

Photographs copyright ©: Robert Aberman/B. Heller/Art Resource, NY:
p. 7; Galen Rowell/Corbis: p. 8; Paul Almasy/Corbis: p. 9; Kerstin Geier;
ABPL/Corbis: p. 11; William J. Dewey: p. 15; Robert Holmes/Corbis:
p. 17; Robert Pickett; Papilio/Corbis: p. 21; Brendan Ryan; ABPL/Corbis:
p. 25; David Reed/Corbis: pp. 26, 33, 42; Christine Osborne/Corbis: pp.
28, 38; Eye Ubiquitous/Corbis: p. 31; Wendy Stone/Liaison International:
pp. 34, 39; Herbert W. Booth III, 1992/Liaison International: p. 36; Trip/L.
Reemer/The Viesti Collection, Inc.: p. 41; Ira Fox: p. 47; Werner Forman
Archive, Art Resource, NY: p. 49; Nik Wheeler/Corbis: p. 53; Richard
Bickel/Corbis: p. 55; J. McLaughlin/Maryknoll Missioners: p. 57.

Library of Congress Cataloging-in-Publication Data

Bessire, Mark.
    Great Zimbabwe / Mark Bessire. — 1st ed.
        p.   cm. — (A first book) (African civilizations)
    Includes bibliographical references and index.
    Summary: A survey of the history and culture of Great Zimbabwe,
the capital of a powerful city-state that flourished in southern Africa
from about 1300 to 1525.
    ISBN 0-531-20285-2
    1. Great Zimbabwe (Extinct city)—Juvenile literature.   2. Shona
(African people)—Zimbabwe—Great Zimbabwe—History—Juvenile
literature.   [1. Great Zimbabwe (Extinct city)]   I. Title.
II. Series.   III. Series: African civilizations.
DT3025.G84B47   1998
968.91'01—dc21   97-31289
                                                                          CIP
                                                                          AC

CONTENTS

INTRODUCTION

Great Zimbabwe (zim-BUB-weh) was a powerful trading *city-state* in southeast Africa that existed from approximately 1300 to 1525. It was located on the highland *plateau* that occupies much of the present-day country of Zimbabwe.

Great Zimbabwe was built by the ancestors of the Shona (SHOH-nah) people. Today 70 percent of the population of modern Zimbabwe—which is named after Great Zimbabwe—is Shona.

THE CAPITAL AND ITS RUINS

The capital city of the Great Zimbabwe city-state, which was itself called Great Zimbabwe, was the largest city in southern Africa at that time. It was a magnificent city, filled with enormous stone buildings.

The exquisite ruins of Great Zimbabwe suggest that it was the grand capital of a powerful city-state.

The ruins of the buildings at the capital—which are known today simply as Great Zimbabwe—can still be explored. They are among the greatest examples of African architecture.

Objects found at the ruins include many items of gold, beautifully decorated weapons, porcelain imported from China, and stone sculptures. The most famous sculptures are column-like stone pillars topped with birds, known as Zimbabwe birds.

One indirect source of information about Great Zimbabwe comes from an empire that rose in the region even as Great Zimbabwe declined, the Mwenemutapa Empire. Part of this empire was located on the Zambezi River, seen here.

These and other finds make it clear that the capital traded with many other African cities and with countries overseas.

DISCOVERING GREAT ZIMBABWE

Three important sources of information provide us with clues about the city-state of Great Zimbabwe. The first is the ruins themselves, which indicate the greatness of the society that built them.

Much archaeological evidence at Great Zimbabwe was carelessly disturbed in the late 1800s.

The second source of information is research by archaeologists—scientists who study how people lived long ago. Unfortunately, treasure hunters and early archaeologists in the late 1800s disturbed the area around the ruins by reckless digging. They destroyed or mixed together a great deal of evidence from the past. Modern archaeologists, who use more careful methods and might have made important discoveries if the ruins had been left intact, have done the next best thing. They have studied evidence from states that existed in the region several centuries earlier than Great Zimbabwe. The most important of these was Mapungubwe (mah-POONG-goob-wee).

Scholars believe that Great Zimbabwe followed in the footsteps of Mapungubwe and earlier trading centers in the region, which had specialized in trading such goods as food, salt, iron, copper, fabrics, and cattle. They believe Great Zimbabwe grew wealthy by controlling trade over the Zimbabwean plateau.

In addition, scholars have identified a few remarks about this region of Africa that were written down by Arab and Portuguese writers in about 1500. These deal mainly with a trading state that rose to power as Great Zimbabwe declined. Called the Mwenemutapa (m-when-a-MOO-tup-uh) Empire, this state may have contributed to the decline of Great Zimbabwe by attracting away its trading partners. These written accounts are useful for understanding how the states that followed Great Zimbabwe continued its trading practices and some of its traditions. However, they do not provide eyewitness accounts of Great Zimbabwe itself.

The builders of Great Zimbabwe are the ancestors of the Shona people, who live in the modern country of Zimbabwe. This Shona woman is a priestess and concerned with spiritual matters. The Shona people believe that the spirits of their ancestors influence daily events.

The third important source of information about Great Zimbabwe is research into the history, religion, and traditions of the Shona people, whose ancestors built Great Zimbabwe. This research takes into account the fact that over the centuries many changes in Shona society may have occurred.

THE IMPORTANCE OF TRADE

Gold was probably the key factor that made Great Zimbabwe much richer and more powerful than its predecessors. Gold was plentiful throughout the Zimbabwean plateau. Great Zimbabwe traded with African merchants who lived along the East African coast. These merchants spoke Swahili, an African language that contains many Arabic words. The east coast of Africa is often called the Swahili Coast because it was dotted with towns established by Swahili traders, all of whom had a broadly similar culture. Like the Arabs, most Swahili were Muslims. They were influenced by Arab culture in many ways.

The Swahili traded with Arab and sometimes Indian and Chinese traders, who traveled across the Indian Ocean to conduct trade in East Africa.

The Swahili traded gold from Great Zimbabwe, as well as goods such as copper, ivory, and animal skins. In return they—and Great Zimbabwe—received glass beads, cloth, porcelain, and other items.

The capital of Great Zimbabwe was the center from which the ruler of Great Zimbabwe controlled trade with the coast. All across the *plateau* smaller settlements collected gold and other trade goods and sent them to the capital. These settlements—about one hundred fifty in all—featured stone buildings similar to those at the capital but smaller.

The grand scale of the capital and its architecture made a powerful statement about the ruler and his state. So impressive was the capital that early European visitors to its ruins were amazed. Great Zimbabwe remains one of the greatest monuments of African civilization.

1 THE RISE OF GREAT ZIMBABWE

More than two thousand years ago, *Bantu* peoples migrated from central Africa and began to settle in eastern and southern Africa. The Bantu who settled between the Limpopo and Zambezi rivers included people of many language groups. They were farmers and herders and tended to settle in large villages close to rivers. They also hunted and gathered wild foods.

The Bantu lived in thatched houses made of wooden poles and earthen walls. This type of house, which is cool in summer and warm in winter, was built at Great Zimbabwe and is still used by many rural Zimbabweans.

Thatched houses, which are well suited to the climate of Zimbabwe, were built in Great Zimbabwe and are often built in rural Zimbabwe today.

EARLY HISTORY

Between A.D. 200 and 1000, trade became an increasingly important part of life for the early Bantu settled near the Zimbabwean plateau. Trade brought together people who lived in different climates in the region and people from distant cultures. They began to specialize in products that they could trade, including salt, pottery, and metal.

Before the end of the tenth century several small settlements along the Limpopo River had developed into important centers for trade in the region and were also trading with the Swahili Coast. The most important of these was Mapungubwe.

Unlike Great Zimbabwe, the ruins of Mapungubwe have never been disturbed by treasure hunters. Archaeologists have been able to learn a great deal about its society and economy from careful excavations at the site. Scholars believe that Great Zimbabwe probably grew to power several centuries later in a manner similar to Mapungubwe. Mapungubwe thus provides many important clues about Great Zimbabwe.

MAPUNGUBWE

It is not known when Mapungubwe was established, but by 1075 it had become a well-organized trading center. It had a strong ruling class that formed the *elite* of the society. The rest of the population were no longer subsistence farmers and herders producing just enough food to survive. They had become blacksmiths, potters, weavers, tool makers, traditional doctors, and traders.

The capital of Mapungubwe and other trading centers were built on and around hills. Most of the

Mapungubwe's power started to decline in roughly 1200, as Great Zimbabwe began to gain power to the north. Above, a Shona woman, whose ancestors founded Great Zimbabwe, uses a mortar and pestle to pound grain.

population lived at the base of the hill. Near the top lived the ruler and the small, wealthy class that made up the ruling elite.

The economy of Mapungubwe was based on cattle. People measured their wealth, power, and status in cattle. The climate of the region could support large cattle herds all year round, so individuals and families became wealthy as their herds grew. Cattle were sometimes used in trade with neighboring societies, many of which eventually became part of Mapungubwe. Mapungubwe's territory and power continued to expand.

As Mapungubwe grew, its ruler appointed lesser chiefs to rule for him in outlying districts and in smaller settlements nearby. In return for being included in Mapungubwe's economy and for being protected by Mapungubwe, these distant chiefs paid tribute—a type of tax paid in food, cattle, metal, or other valuables—to the ruler.

When Mapungubwe began to trade with the Swahili Coast, the ruling elite gained access to such imported luxuries as glass beads, which had never been seen in the region before. Luxury goods were symbols of wealth and status. They were controlled by the ruler, who could give them to allies and neighboring chiefs in return for their loyalty. The people of the region became increasingly dependent on international trade and on the centralized government at Mapungubwe.

Among the items discovered by scientists at Mapungubwe are locally produced objects decorated with gold foil. The most famous of these is a sculpture of a rhinoceros. Gold was probably the item most sought after by the Swahili traders, followed by ivory, rhinoceros horn, and other animal products. But among the Bantu, for whom wealth was measured in cattle, gold was of lesser interest.

THE RISE OF GREAT ZIMBABWE

Mapungubwe's power began to decline in about 1200, just as Great Zimbabwe began to rise farther north. At the same time the trade routes of the Swahili traders also shifted northward. This suggests that Great Zimbabwe may have overtaken Mapungubwe as the leading gold supplier to the Swahili traders.

The rise of Great Zimbabwe occurred at the same time as the Swahili were improving their own trade networks. The capital was built where the Great Zimbabwe ruins are found today. The Swahili city of Kilwa became a key port from which gold, ivory, skins, and other products were exported.

GEOGRAPHY

The physical environment was an important factor in the success and growth of Great Zimbabwe. The capital was built on the eastern edge of the Zimbabwean plateau, the side closest to the East African coast. The plateau is a highland area with a healthful climate, excellent summer grazing for cattle, and several rich gold deposits.

To the west, the plateau gives way to desert. To the east, south, and north, it drops down steeply into lowlands that have dense vegetation. During the summer the lowlands are infested by mosquitoes that carry *malaria* and by tsetse flies, which cause sleeping sickness in humans and can kill cattle. In the winter, when the plateau is cold and dry, the tsetse flies disappear, and the threat of malaria is reduced in the lowlands. This allows people to descend to graze their cattle there, where the grass is still green, and to hunt.

The landscape of the Zimbabwean plateau is dotted with rocky outcrops, called *kopjes.*

The Zimbabwean plateau has a variety of natural environments and features. Grasslands with good grazing for cattle are mixed with areas of fertile soil for farming and the forested savanna favored by wild animals. It is ideal for raising cattle, farming, and hunting. Farming depends on good rains, however, and the plateau's rainfall is unreliable. Every five years or so a terrible drought occurs.

The plateau is dotted with rocky hills called *kopjes* and other dome-like hills of granite. Reefs of gold-bearing rock often occur close to the surface, where they can be mined easily. Rivers cutting through these reefs also wash out the gold. This alluvial gold—gold carried away by water—can be panned.

Archaeologists believe that the capital of Great Zimbabwe exploited these favorable factors and came to dominate outlying districts and neighboring areas as Mapungubwe had done before it.

THE BUILDING OF GREAT ZIMBABWE

At its peak of power the capital of Great Zimbabwe was the largest city in southeastern Africa. It had a population of between 15,000 and 18,000. Never before in the region had so many people been drawn together under one economic and political system.

To feed the city's population, food was probably sent from outlying areas. Local chiefs were responsible for collecting food and other items of tribute from their communities and sending these to the capital. These local leaders, together with those who assisted the ruler in the capital, made up the ruling elite.

The majority of the population lived by farming

and herding during the wet season. During the dry season they were probably required to mine gold and hunt as part of their tribute to the capital.

The capital and the settlements that fell under its control—roughly one hundred fifty—all had extensive stone structures. The Shona today call each of these stone constructions *dzimbahwe*, meaning the court, home, or grave of a chief. *Madzimbahwe* is the plural form of *dzimbahwe*, and the phrase *dzimba dza mabwe* is translated as "house of stone." The *madzimbahwe* scattered throughout the state of Great Zimbabwe were the centers of government and homes of the ruling elite. They were far more impressive than those built earlier at Mapungubwe.

BUILDING IN STONE

The earliest stone buildings at the capital of Great Zimbabwe were built in about 1300. The granite domes in the region provided building material. The surface layers of the granite domes break up and peel off through decades of exposure to heat, cold, and rain. This is known as onion-peel weathering, because the effect is much like peeling layers

The domed granite hills on the plateau provided the building material for the *madzimbahwe* occupied by the elite of Great Zimbabwe. Many *madzimbahwe* were built at the top of granite hills and around natural boulders.

The highest section of wall at Great Zimbabwe reaches 35 feet (11.5 m) in height.

from an onion. The broken granite slabs are about the thickness of modern bricks and can easily be shaped by chipping off their irregular edges.

The weathering process can be speeded up. First, a fire is built on top of the granite, then water is poured on the hot granite to cool it rapidly. This shatters the rock. The rough slabs can then be broken into convenient sizes for carrying to the building site.

The stone walls were strong and durable, but they had to be very wide at the base to support their weight. Some walls at the ruins of Great Zimbabwe are 35 feet (11.5 m) high and half that width at the base. The hidden center of the walls was composed of rubble.

The walls built later at Great Zimbabwe were built better than the earlier ones. The stones in the later walls are more regular in size and shape and lie in straighter and more tightly packed rows. Some walls are decorated with patterns, including zigzag, herringbone, and check designs. These were formed by placing the stones at angles or recessing alternate stones. Another form of decoration was the use of darker, contrasting stones. Scholars now believe that each of these patterns had a special symbolic meaning.

DAGA

Often both the stone surfaces of the buildings and their stone-paved floors were covered with a finishing layer of clay cement called *daga* (DUG-ah).

Daga, which is still used by the rural Shona people today to cover their walls and floors, consists of mud, cattle dung, and other substances. The dung has a high ammonia content, which acts as an antiseptic and also prevents seeds from germinating. *Daga* is effective for keeping out rain and is a good insulator against both heat and cold. It

Many of the bare stone surfaces seen at Great Zimbabwe today were once covered with *daga* that was painted or polished. A Shona house demonstrates that *daga* can be easily molded, painted, and polished.

is easily smoothed by hand when it is applied wet, and it can be painted with such natural paints as colored earth. On the floor, *daga* creates a hard and hygienic surface that is easily cleaned. Some floors at Great Zimbabwe were up to 18 inches (45 cm) thick.

Close to the Great Zimbabwe ruins, archaeologists have found huge pits where the clay for *daga* was collected. Many of the surfaces of the ruins were once probably covered in *daga* and polished or painted with geometric designs.

HOUSES

A family *homestead* at the capital consisted of several *daga* houses. Family members had their own separate dwellings. Among the elite, these dwellings were linked by low stone walls to form a homestead. Each homestead, in turn, was linked to other homesteads by similar walls. These shared walls provided privacy, surfaces for decoration, and protection against bad weather and wild animals

Together, several family homesteads made up a compound or *enclosure*. Each enclosure had its own external wall and a large open space in the center of the buildings. Many enclosures of various sizes made up the capital city of Great Zimbabwe. Most scholars believe that the small stone enclosures were occupied by members of the ruling elite.

It is the very large structures at Great Zimbabwe, however, that are the most impressive and fascinating. These are the Great Enclosure in the valley of Great Zimbabwe, and the Hill Site, which overlooks it.

3 THE HILL SITE

The Hill Site is built on the top of a steep granite mountain. It is an imposing setting, difficult to reach, and it provides protection and an excellent view of the valley. The mountain is easily climbed from only one side, and even then the journey is hard, although it has been eased by a system of stone-walled terraces.

Many smaller enclosures—some very private, others linked by passageways—have been created by a network of stone walls that divides the hilltop. These small areas were made level with *daga*, forming terraces at several levels. Stone pathways led to various small enclosures, to secret passage-

A network of narrow pathways connects the numerous smaller enclosures found on the Hill Site at Great Zimbabwe.

ways, and to paths down to the valley.

The crest of the hill is surrounded by massive stone walls that are built over and around the boulders. Built into the hilltop are two large enclosures: the Western and Eastern Enclosures.

THE WESTERN ENCLOSURE

The main pathway to the hilltop begins in the valley with an impressive gateway. From there the path leads up the mountain toward massive walls, which are decorated on top with *monoliths* and small stone towers. An entrance through the walls leads into the Western Enclosure, a large and relatively public space.

The remains of the oldest buildings at Great Zimbabwe have been found in the Western Enclosure, suggesting that it was occupied earliest. These buildings are *daga* structures dating back to the eleventh and twelfth centuries—well before the first stone walls. Within the Western Enclosure were as many as fourteen dwellings and an open court. An area appears to have been set aside for worship; it contains a decorated, altar-like platform, and one of the famous Zimbabwe birds was found nearby. Archaeologists have also discovered gold fragments in the Western Enclosure.

The evidence suggests that the Western Enclosure was an early *dzimbahwe*, much like the hilltop residence of the ruler of Mapungubwe. Scholars believe that the first ruler of Great Zimbabwe lived

The walls around the Western Enclosure are topped with turrets and monoliths, the stone structures sticking up from the wall.

here, but they disagree over whether later rulers continued to live here. Some think these other rulers moved to the Great Enclosure in the valley, leaving the Western Enclosure available for other uses.

THE EASTERN ENCLOSURE

At the easternmost side of the hilltop—about 200 feet (70 m) from the Western Enclosure—is the Eastern Enclosure. It is reached by pathways through a number of other, smaller enclosures. The

The Eastern Enclosure is thought to have been a place of worship.

route is narrow and windy, and the enclosure itself is small and sheltered, unlike the open atmosphere of the Western Enclosure. This suggests that the Eastern Enclosure was a particularly private area, suitable for the private or even secret activities of a powerful ruler or religious leader. The Eastern Enclosure even has an underground passage, which a ruler or priest could have used as a secret entrance, or to appear suddenly as if by magic.

No evidence of houses or household utensils has been found in the Eastern Enclosure; however, six of the seven stone Zimbabwe birds found on the hill were in the Eastern Enclosure. They had probably been set up on altars, stone platforms decorated with painted *daga*. Also found were several stone bowls with intricate carvings, which were probably used in religious ceremonies. Taken together, this evidence suggests that the Eastern Enclosure was a site for worship—probably the worship of the ruler's ancestors, who were represented as birds. Here either the ruler, or his *spirit medium*, or both prayed and made offerings to the royal ancestors for rain and prosperity.

A balcony on the crest of the Hill Site

Above the Eastern Enclosure is a natural balcony embedded in the rocks overlooking the valley. Its use is unknown. Below the Eastern Enclosure is a shallow cave that probably played a religious role related to the shrine area above. Drums played in this cave would have been heard throughout the valley. Similar features have been found at other sites that were built after Great Zimbabwe's decline.

4 THE GREAT ENCLOSURE

The valley below the Hill Site is filled with ruins, but the Great Enclosure dominates the site.

The Great Enclosure is similar in design to many others in the valley but was built on a far grander scale. One archaeologist has estimated that it contains more stonework than the rest of the ruins combined. The outer wall is more than 800 feet (244 m) long, and the inner area is 70 feet (21 m) across and has four entrances.

Inside are several smaller enclosures that once contained dwellings. These small structures may have been inhabited by the ruler, his wives, children, and other members of the elite. Some scholars

The Great Enclosure is surrounded by the ruins of numerous smaller enclosures, which are spread out over the valley.

believe the Great Enclosure was the exclusive home of the ruler's first wife. Others think it may have been used as a center for the state's young women, who lived there and attended an initiation school to learn about their culture and prepare for marriage and motherhood. The Great Enclosure also contains the two most famous—and puzzling—features of the ruins: the parallel passage and the conical tower.

THE PARALLEL PASSAGE
The parallel passage was created when the high, outer wall of the Great Enclosure was built. Just inside the outer wall, on the northwest side of the

The parallel passage inside the Great Enclosure

Great Enclosure, is another, older wall. The newer, outer wall is the highest and widest in the structure.

From the entrance, the parallel passage curves out of sight toward the conical tower at the back of the Great Enclosure. The walls tower above anyone walking down the passage. The floor is also made of stone, creating the sense of being surrounded by stone on three sides—although the stones would once have been plastered with *daga*.

Users of the parallel passage would have been invisible to anyone inside or outside the Great Enclosure. Some scholars believe that the passage provided a way for members of the elite to reach the tower.

THE CONICAL TOWER

The conical tower, a solid tower, tapers from bottom to top. It reaches the same height as the outer wall behind it—about 35 feet (11.5 m). It has a diameter of 18 feet (6 m). It was probably built in the fifteenth century, during the height of Great Zimbabwe's power. Next to the conical tower is a large open area containing a raised stepped platform, and nearby is a smaller but similar tower. The design of the tower and the skillful building technique make it one of the highlights of the ruins at the capital.

Because scholars have been unable to find any practical use for this tower, they believe it may have been either a royal symbol or a religious shrine. It may represent a granary—the large storage containers for grain that were (and still are) built by the Shona. It could, therefore, have been a religious symbol for the idea that the ruler, working together with his ancestors, was responsible for making the rain that produced abundant harvests, which filled the granaries of the people. Four smaller enclosures of a similar date, outside the Great Enclosure, also have smaller towers and platforms.

The conical tower inside the Great Enclosure

An entrance in a wall shows how steps were created by continuing the rows of stone that form the walls. Like all the walls at Great Zimbabwe, the design favors curved lines rather than straight.

The top of the tower and the outer wall behind it were both decorated with a zigzag pattern. In addition, monoliths also decorated both the outer wall and the platform next to the conical tower. These features suggest that this part of the Great Enclosure was sacred. Scholars believe that the monoliths represent bulls' horns. The Shona liken their chiefs to bulls, who both protect their herd and enlarge it by fertilizing the cows. Like a bull, the chief is the leader and protector of his followers, and he plays a vital role in the fertility of everything that lives off the land because he brings the rain required to survive, grow, and reproduce. The monoliths may have been symbols of these functions of the ruler of Great Zimbabwe.

WALLS AS STATEMENTS OF POWER

Unlike other city walls used for defense, which have certain elements to help soldiers fight or see the enemy from far away, the walls at Great Zimbabwe supply no clues to suggest that the city had a large army or many weapons. Rather, all the major enclosures seem designed to separate the people inside—probably members of the elite—

from the people outside. The grand walls of the major sites make a forceful statement of the greatness and wealth of the capital. They must have been very impressive to any foreign visitor or to the ordinary people of the state who lived in outlying areas.

The walls powerfully suggest that the ruler controlled a huge labor force, including many skilled craftspeople. Of course, the ability to control the building of Great Zimbabwe was just one element of his power. He headed a centralized government that dominated a large area and controlled trade throughout the region and with the outside world. He also played a key religious role in society.

5 TRADE AND RELIGION

The buildings of Great Zimbabwe make clear that its ruling elite had perfected the recipe that had made the earlier state of Mapungubwe a great center of trade. This enabled the people of Great Zimbabwe to build the largest and grandest city ever seen in this part of Africa.

TRADE

There is little doubt among scholars that the gold trade with the Swahili Coast was what made Great Zimbabwe great. In the fourteenth century the city of Kilwa began to use gold as an international currency for trade. This and other factors increased the demand for gold, which Great Zimbabwe supplied.

At Great Zimbabwe, however, gold was used only by the ruling elite, as decoration, and because of its limited practical use it had little local value. In return for gold, Great Zimbabwe received glass beads, porcelain, and other luxury items that were relatively inexpensive in the countries where they were produced. Thus, the ruling elite of Great Zimbabwe and the Swahili traders both gave up things they valued little.

The ruler of Great Zimbabwe used the imported luxuries as signs of his status and power, and he gave some of them to members of the elite as rewards. Some imports may have been traded for cattle, which remained the people's measure of wealth.

THE RULER'S RELIGIOUS ROLE

The ruler's religious role was probably as important as his political and economic roles. There is no clear archaeological evidence of this, but Shona religious traditions today provide clues to what a ruler's religious functions might have been in the past.

The Shona believe that their ancestors, or *mudzimu*, must be remembered in daily life and honored through special rituals. If the ancestors

One of the most important objects used by modern Shona *masvikiro* to contact the spirit world is a container filled with oil. Similar containers were decorated with metal wire of different colors in Great Zimbabwe, where metal and beads were both considered luxuries.

are respected in this way, they watch over the family and guarantee its well-being. If the ancestors are neglected or offended, however, they can bring misfortune and disaster. The power of an ancestral spirit is related to the power and status of that person in life. For this reason, the ancestors of chiefs are particularly important. They are responsible for the well-being of the entire community. Living chiefs play a vital role in communicating with their ancestors.

According to Shona beliefs, the ancestral spirits live in the earth. God, called Mwari in Shona, lives in the sky and makes rain. The spirits of dead chiefs are the mediums, or go-betweens, between Mwari and the world of the living. The living chief asks his ancestors to approach Mwari on behalf of the community, especially to ask for rain. He is assisted by a spirit medium, or diviner—known in Shona as a *svikiro* (plural *masvikiro*)—who is an expert at communicating with the spirits. A *svikiro* is able to become possessed by a spirit, meaning that the spirit enters the medium's body, takes control of it, and speaks through the medium.

It is likely that the ruler of Great Zimbabwe, like Shona chiefs today, was responsible for the relationship between the living community and the spirit world, and that spirit mediums were active in court life, rainmaking, and the election of new chiefs.

Symbols of three important animals that are connected with rain in Shona belief today are all found at Great Zimbabwe: the bird, the bull, and the snake. The Shona regard the snake as a messenger between the earth and the spirit world below. Birds, particularly the eagle, are able to

A stone sculpture found at Great Zimbabwe. The wings on its back may refer to the idea of a spiritual messenger who is able to fly to heaven to ask Mwari to bring rain.

travel between the earth and the sky, where Mwari lives. The bull symbolizes the chief's power and prosperity, which are in turn linked to his ability to ensure rain. These symbols suggest that religious ideas relating to rain were a key factor in the life of Great Zimbabwe.

The Zimbabwe birds—seven found on the hill and one in the valley—are all about 14 inches (36 cm) high and carved on top of pillars. Each bird is unique: some have human features, some are standing, others are seated. We may never know exactly what these differences mean, but it is probable that the birds were regarded as eagles, which are known in Shona as "birds of heaven." They were probably regarded as the ruler's ancestors, who carried his prayers for rain to Mwari, and they were inserted into stone walls or placed on top of altars covered with *daga*.

THE DECLINE OF GREAT ZIMBABWE

Great Zimbabwe prospered from 1300 to 1450, and then began to decline—probably because of shortages of natural resources, drought, political problems, and competition from new settlements.

As Great Zimbabwe grew, the human and cattle population would have increased greatly. This may have led to shortages of food and grazing that would have become critical in time of drought. Since the ruler was responsible for bringing rain, drought could also have created a political crisis in which the people might have said that the ruler was a failure and a fraud.

Perhaps Great Zimbabwe's gold supply failed because the mines became worked out, or perhaps a new gold supplier began to draw the Swahili traders away—just as Great Zimbabwe had done earlier to Mapungubwe.

As the state grew, increasing distances between the capital and its farthest settlements may have resulted in less and less contact between the two. Some smaller settlements and elite families did break away from the state. They had probably become wealthy enough to run their own affairs and even become competitors of Great Zimbabwe. These breakaway settlements carried on much of the culture and traditions of Great Zimbabwe for centuries.

One breakaway group, the Torwa, migrated west to the Khami River around 1450—nearly 50 years before people began to desert the capital. Their city resembled Great Zimbabwe but was smaller. Their buildings were more decorative and had better drainage systems. Some even had underground entrance tunnels.

Another breakaway Shona group, the Karanga people, founded a trading state near the Zambezi River on the northern edge of the Zimbabwean plateau in about 1400. Their leader was given the honorary title Mwene Mutapa, meaning "one who explores" or "one who pillages," a title adopted by his successors. He established the Mwenemutapa Empire, which may have played a role in the decline of Great Zimbabwe.

Mwene Mutapa's descendants made contact with the Portuguese in 1500. At this time the Portuguese were attempting to take control of the Swahili Coast and the gold trade on the Zimbabwe plateau. They settled along the Zambezi River and traded with the Mwenemutapa Empire, which now controlled many of the areas previously ruled by Great Zimbabwe. The Portuguese, however, were disappointed at the amount of gold obtained from Mwenemutapa. New sources of gold had recently been discovered in the

A view of the Zambezi River. The Portuguese made contact with the Mwenemutapa Empire, established by the Karanga people who had broken away from Great Zimbabwe. The Portuguese established several trading settlements along the Zambezi River.

Americas. Attention shifted away from the Zimbabwean plateau, and the once great capitals there declined.

THE LEGACY OF GREAT ZIMBABWE

In the late nineteenth century the Shona descendants of the people of Great Zimbabwe and its breakaway states faced a great new challenge: British colonialism. The centuries that had passed since Great Zimbabwe's peak had not erased its fame as a source of gold. British leaders were convinced that the Zimbabwean plateau was fabulously rich, and they decided to seize the region and make it a British territory. In 1895 the British colony was named Rhodesia, after Cecil John Rhodes, a mining millionaire who had persuaded the British government to take an interest in the region.

The British refused to believe that Great Zimbabwe had been created by the ancestors of the

In the late 1800s the land once known as Great Zimbabwe was colonized by the British, who named it Rhodesia. The beautiful falls on the Zambezi River, Mosi-oa-Tunya ("the smoke that thunders") was renamed Victoria Falls after Queen Victoria.

Shona, whom they wrongly regarded as incapable of having built a powerful trading state and a magnificent capital. They thought Great Zimbabwe had been built by an ancient culture from biblical times. The British also failed to understand how the gold had been obtained: mined by hand from numerous reefs scattered all over the plateau. They had hoped to find an abundant supply of gold close to the surface. It soon became clear that this would not happen. The colony of Rhodesia was a disappointment, but the British did not give up their control.

A Shona uprising against the British in 1896 shows how the Shona religion, which had probably been a key factor in the Great Zimbabwe state, still played a powerful political role. The *masvikiro* of the Shona proclaimed that they had received messages from great Shona ancestors urging the Shona to fight the British. The Shona did. The British put down the 1896 uprising and kept control of Rhodesia.

In 1964 the British were prepared to let Rhodesia become an independent, democratic country. But many white Rhodesians refused to allow this to happen because democracy would have meant that the black majority of Rhodesia would gain control of

When Rhodesia became the independent country of Zimbabwe in 1980, people honored the great *masvikiro* who had urged them to resist both the British and, later, the Rhodesian government. The portrait on the top of this woman's skirt is of Nehanda, a *svikiro* during the 1896 uprising.

the country. Instead, the white Rhodesians rebelled against Britain and continued to govern Rhodesia as a white-ruled state until 1980.

The Rhodesian government also refused to recognize that Great Zimbabwe had been built by Shona ancestors. As more and more scientific evidence came to light proving that Great Zimbabwe was an ancient Shona city, the Rhodesian government passed laws forbidding that knowledge to be stated as fact. The government feared that if the truth were known, people might realize that the black people of the country had a great cultural heritage and had long ago proven themselves capable of running a powerful state.

Great Zimbabwe remained a powerful force despite the many centuries that had passed since its fall. The blacks of Rhodesia were well aware of this power of Great Zimbabwe as a symbol of their heritage, and they were determined to win control of their country. When they failed to do so through peaceful discussions, they turned to armed warfare. They finally defeated the white Rhodesians and held democratic elections in 1980.

The Shona-dominated political party won control of the government. The newly independent country was renamed Zimbabwe in honor of the civilization of Great Zimbabwe, built by the ancestors of the Shona. The national symbol became a Zimbabwe bird, and the national flag was designed with a Zimbabwe bird as the centerpiece.

The legacy of Great Zimbabwe, suppressed by the former white government, had emerged once again to play a leading role in national life.

TIMELINE

A.D. c.1000	Ancestors of the Shona arrive on Zimbabwean plateau
c. 1075	Mapungubwe becomes important trading center
c. 1250-1300	Decline of Mapungubwe
c. 1270-1290	First major building projects at Great Zimbabwe
c. 1300-1450	Great Zimbabwe reaches the height of its power; the Hill Site and Great Enclosure are built
c. 1400	Mwenemutapa Empire established on the Zambezi River
c. 1500	Great Zimbabwe abandoned; Portuguese arrive on Swahili Coast; Mwenemutapa encounters Portuguese
1889	Cecil Rhodes's British South Africa Company receives British royal charter to control Mashona territory
1895	Cecil Rhodes names territory Rhodesia
1896	Uprising of Shona and Ndebele against the British
1914	Period of rule by the British South Africa Company ends
1923	Territory becomes self-governing British colony of Southern Rhodesia
1932	Shona and Ndebele leaders form the African National Congress of Southern Rhodesia to challenge colonial rule
1965	White government declares independence and forms the Republic of Rhodesia, which is internationally isolated
1980	Democratic elections; Robert Mugabe, a Shona leader, is elected the first prime minister of Zimbabwe

GLOSSARY

Bantu group of peoples who occupy central, eastern, and southern Africa and speak one of many Bantu languages

city-state state composed of a city and its surrounding territory

daga cement-like substance consisting of mud, cattle dung, and other substances

dzimbahwe (plural: *madzimbahwe*) stone building that serves as a court, home, or grave of kings

elite a small group having high social standing

enclosure connected group of homesteads

homestead a group of several *daga* houses for a family

malaria disease characterized by chills and fever, transmitted by mosquito bite

monolith single large stone, often in the form of a column

mudzimu ancestral spirits of the Shona people

plateau large and relatively flat area of land that is raised sharply above nearby land on at least one side

spirit medium person endowed with ability to communicate with the spirits of ancestors

svikiro (plural: *masvikiro*) spirit medium

FOR FURTHER READING

Avi-Yonah, Michael. *Dig This: How Archaeologists Uncover Our Past*. Minneapolis, MN: Runestone Press, 1993.

Garlake, P. S. *Great Zimbabwe*. New York: Stein and Day, 1973.

McIntosh, Jane. *Archaeology*. Eyewitness Books. New York: Knopf, 1994.

Van Wyk, Gary, and Robert Johnson, Jr. *Shona*. New York: Rosen Publishing Group, 1995.

WEB SITES
Due to the changeable nature of the Internet, sites appear and disappear very quickly. Internet addresses must be entered with capital and lowercase letters exactly as they appear.

Great Zimbabwe from Virtual Zimbabwe: http://www.unicc.org/untpdc/incubator/zwe/tphar/vrz10011.htm

Great Zimbabwe page: http://csf.colorado.edu/ipe/zimbabwe_seminar/madzimbabwe.html

The Zimbabwe Network—Great Zimbabwe: http://www1.zimbabwe.net/about/great_zimbabwe/

INDEX

ABOUT THE AUTHOR

Mark Bessire is an academic dean at Harvard University and works at the Harvard University Art Museums. He was a recent Fulbright Fellow in Museum Studies at the Sukuma Museum in Tanzania. He received an M.B.A. from Columbia University and an M.A. in Art History from Hunter College of the City University of New York. He was also a Helena Rubinstein Fellow at the Whitney Museum of American Art in New York.